A
Boy's
Journal

A Boy's Journal

Yi Ding

PARTRIDGE
A Penguin Random House Company

ISBN: Softcover   978-1-4828-3160-3
             eBook   978-1-4828-3161-0

Print information available on the last page.

To order additional copies of this book, contact
Toll Free 800 101 2657 (Singapore)
Toll Free 1 800 81 7340 (Malaysia)
orders.singapore@partridgepublishing.com

www.partridgepublishing.com/singapore

Before you read this journal, you may *need* to know: My name is Yi Ding, now a *fifth* grade student in China. I have a big family: Dad, Mom, grandparents, aunt, uncle, and my younger cousin. I have a good friend whose nickname is Peekaboo.

Saturday, January 25, 2014

Well, I don't think this is a good start for my new journal. I just came to Singapore on vacation and Mom suddenly said I need to study in one of Singapore school because it can improve my English. My English is already very good in China. And I don't think I'll have a good time here. I don't know why--I just don't feel good!

I finally agreed to go to school in Singapore next Monday when Mom offered me ten bucks a day. Anyway, there's still a Sunday for relaxing.

Mom was talking about future with me today, and I'm only worrying about one thing thirty years later: since so many kids want to be scientists, I think the jobs would be kind of unbalancing in the future....

Mom says if I don't study at the Singapore school, I'll never become a translator. But I don't think it that way.

Monday, January 27, 2014

Today is the first day of school. The school isn't that bad. The teachers were quite good. Only thing I felt embarrassing is that I wore the wrong school shorts.

When I came back home from school, I witnessed a tragic incident: Dad was tripping over one of those slippers in the bedroom and broke his glasses.

Dad and I also went downstairs to play soccer this afternoon. It was fun, and Dad showed me some cool moves. I got tired very fast and my hair was completely wet. But Dad wasn't tired at all—he only got tired when shopping with Mom.

At night, I asked Mom for the ten bucks. She seemed very reluctant, but a deal is a deal. So she pulled ten dollars out of her wallet. I took it without hesitation to prevent Mom from making a second thought.

Wednesday, January 29, 2014

I didn't bring the textbook of Social Study today. Well, I guess if you're a new student in the school, you might have some privileges. Believe it or not, the teacher didn't scold me!

Wednesday, February 5, 2014

The school had a great concert about Chinese New Year yesterday. Things started to go out of control when a man wearing a mask was throwing candy at us. Within two seconds, the whole school went totally crazy. And that's when kids turned evil and started robbing all the candy from him.

Monday, February 10, 2014

I think teachers are making schools really boring..

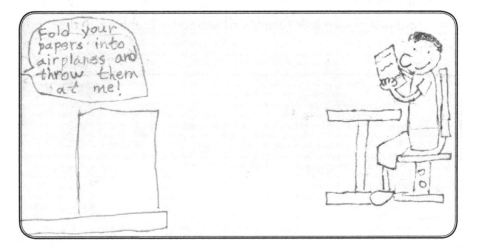

If I were a teacher, I would make the class really fun...

But that might end up in a mess..

Thursday, February 13, 2014

I am planning to build a Lego city, but I'm just stuck with building the mall.

Friday, February 14, 2014

Good news. Mom finally let me go back to China after nearly one month of my insistence. Thanks the teachers in Singapore, they are so nice! They sure understand me more than Mom did.

Sunday, February 16, 2014

I'm in China now, and the winter holidays here were almost over. Yesterday when we were at the airport, the officer who was checking our passports looked very puzzled. I guess it was because Dad wasn't wearing glasses.

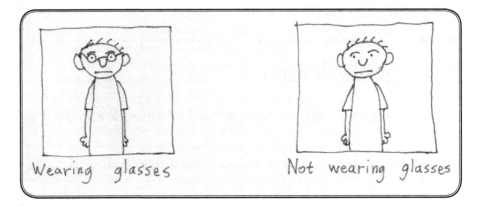

Wearing glasses   Not wearing glasses

Monday, February 17, 2014

Today is the first day of school in China. I rode the school bus to school. I have one friend who was also on the school bus. I usually call him 'Peekaboo'. His behavior sure matches his nickname.

Thursday, February 20, 2014

One thing you must note about our class is that we usually make lots of noise. Our form teacher tried very hard to stop our class from turning into a marketplace. But that's hard to call it a success when you can clearly hear the noise out of the school.

Tuesday, February 25, 2014

I have a good reason to complain about my seat in the classroom. It is freezing cold today, and I found my seat is far away from the radiators.

There was a heavy rain today, and well, I hate rainy days. Let's get to the point, we usually queue up to get on the school bus, and often use our schoolbags to reserve the place for us before the bus arrives. This afternoon I threw my schoolbag on the ground as usual. But this was a terrible mistake—how could I threw my schoolbag on an after-rain ground?! When I came back, I cannot believe my eyes--the other guys used stones to reserve!

In the end, not surprisingly all I got is a wet schoolbag.

Monday, March 3, 2014

Nothing new happened today. It's just that Dad had downloaded "Skype" on his phone, so he can talk to Mom. At the first try on the Skype, do you wonder what the first thing Mom said was?

Monday, March 9, 2014

Our music teacher asked us to buy a melodica, a music instrument that looks like a mini-piano. But she must have regretted doing it since we made it a total disaster. Some guys even play the melodica in other classes.

Our science teacher, well, wanted us to do things like making fungi grow on bread. I did succeed, but I just couldn't get close to the fungi. I guess I would pass out upon that overwhelming stench.

Friday, March 28, 2014

Mom came to China to see us this week, and that is why I didn't write the journal these days. Good thing is I'm ten years old now. The tenth birthday is quite a big birthday for a boy, but I didn't expect it to be that good. Besides the presents, Dad, Mom and I had lunch in the Pizza hut near our home—pizza is one of my favorite foods. I was completely full when we went out of the Pizza hut.

Sunday, April 6, 2014

I spent this weekend in Patrick's house. How do I describe the feeling of my stay there? A combination of happy and boring. First, Patrick was out yesterday, and the only funny thing to play in the house was spinners. Well, it is hard to say that is "fun".

Later, the computer crashed when Patrick came back home.

The happy part is that, I found a big box of toys with Patrick today. They were old ones, and had been put somewhere around the house long time ago. To us, it's a game of treasure hunt!

Sunday, April 20, 2014

I created a talking game at school this week. My friends and I played by speaking words to fight an imaginary war (Of course, you need a very good memory). It became so popular at school that even my friend's mom wanted to join in. My friend made her to pay 5 bucks first for admission, but her new kingdom was destroyed in no time.

I must admit that sometimes the game was crazily made-up, like a T-50 fighter crashed into a torpedo bomber.

Friday, April 25, 2014

Recently peekaboo and I found some wild strawberries. They were quite delicious, but I was afraid that peekaboo might think about something like 'fruit bomb".

Soon it will not be a problem at all. The school gardener is going to mow the lawn. It is a good news for me, but definitely a bad news for grasshoppers.

Sunday, May 11, 2014

We have a bunch of things going on this week. First it was the gecko incident. Monday, when we were having recess, someone just spotted a gecko. Peekaboo and I quickly jumped into action, of course. I caught the gecko at last, but then it suddenly bit my finger.

I was really afraid, so I shook it off. OK, I didn't caught it, and that bite left me shuddering the whole morning.

Second, I learned a lesson on the school bus and would like to share with you: NEVER sit behind a bus driver. Otherwise, you will be the first to bump into the someone's seat when there is an emergency brake.

Wednesday, May 21, 2014

You remember the melodica I usually bring to the music class? We didn't use it recently, so I almost forgot it today.

To me, a melodica is also a great anti-bully weapon.

You might have found that I wrote little about my home recently. That's because there was nothing interesting that happened at home. A bit boring for me...

Wednesday, June 11, 2014

I have more and more homework these days, so I don't have much time to write the journal now. Anyway, I finished building my Lego house. But I might have forgotten something...

Thursday, July 31, 2014

Forgive me that I haven't written the journal for a month. I have been staying with Dad and Mom in Singapore and just came back. Now I'm in Patrick's house. Dad said he had a very good time in Singapore, but I doubt it. All I remember is Dad's sensitive nose.

Patrick had just lost a tooth, but he got nothing from the tooth fairy. I think I know why.

Saturday, August 2, 2014

Today my aunt and uncle brought me and Patrick out to do some shopping. After shopping, we went to a restaurant to have lunch. It's really boring to wait in a long queue outside the restaurant. So my uncle let us play games on his cellphone. Well, play boring games at a boring time.

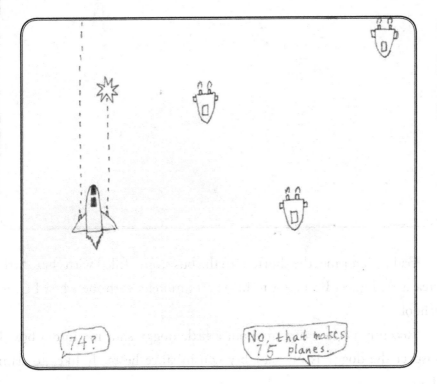

No surprise that we finally quitted the game.

Thursday, August 21, 2014

The past summer holidays were so good for me that I almost forget to write the journal. I realize it until the holidays are nearly over.

The summer is almost ending, now there is a SERIOUS problem, caterpillars. Many of them hang down from trees, here and there. It's really disgusting to get a caterpillar on your face by accident.

Bad luck for me, the shortcut to the bus stop is filled with these little creatures. I guess I'd better to bring an umbrella with me when I go to school.

Recently I had a dream about a little doggy shut me into a box. I suspect the doggy is my naughty cousin since he really likes to slam doors.

Thursday, September 4, 2014

Today is the fourth day of school. At school, there are many caterpillars on the trees, and some have turned into moths or butterflies. The bad thing is, there are so many of them that I need to be very careful with every step.

Monday, September 22, 2014

I don't think I will write a long journal today, because I'm right in the middle of an English pop quiz. You might ask me why I'm writing the journal in the class. The answer is obvious: I have nothing to do and nowhere to go after finishing my paper, and it is really boring to watch other students doing theirs.

I had a bump on my head because I fell on the ground. I don't feel the pain, but worry about that I might have some teeny weeny changes in my brain.

Thursday, October 9, 2014

Today we were playing downstairs of our classroom at school. Suddenly, the little sister of my classmate John, came to chase him for fun. It was really fun to watch a little girl chasing a fifth-grade boy. Well, John's little sister left soon. Just as John started to worry about her, she brought two friends to join the chase game. It ended up with nearly a whole class of little girls and boys chased John in the playground.

Peekaboo and I today poked a beehive in a bush with a stick. Luckily no bee came out of the beehive. We two must have acted like idiots.

Monday, October 27, 2014

I read my old diaries during my second grade days, and really wondered what I was thinking at that time.

> Blue team chased the enemy all the way down the hill. The enemy rolled down the hill. Boom!!! A bomb crashed them. "Wow." said the blue team. "There's another boat," a solider said, "It's the enemy's boat." And the machine was broke. The blue team is fighting.

Peekaboo found bamboo woods recently, and he wants to make a secret house there. I don't like this idea, because of the hays in front of the bamboo woods. Every time I step on it, it sounds like stepping on dog poo.

Friday, October 31, 2014

We also had a Halloween party here in China. Patrick also joined us, and he attempted to eat all the chocolates. Well, he failed. I made a mistake to put all the leftover chocolates into the candy bag. A minute later, all the candies became sticky.

Monday, November 3, 2014

Peekaboo and I found a big pit yesterday, because we fell right into it. We were trying to climb up with a stick. The stick flew away when I pull it—I guess that is because the soils were too soft. We finally got out by grasping the rocks with bare hands.

Remember I said that I hate rainy days? It's not always so. Our teacher asked us to write an essay about leaves today. But it rained, and all the leaves got covered in mud. It will be a good excuse for not writing the essay today.

One of my classmates broke his hand. Everyone says he is lucky to have no homework. I don't think so, because that also means no video games for a month at least.

Sunday, November 9, 2014

I found that in China, English learning is really boring. You just have a look at the homework we need to do, and you will know what I'm talking about.

> What's your favourite food?
>
> My favourite food is pizza.
>
> What's your favourite drink?
>
> My favourite drink is sprite.
>
> Are your favourite food and drink healthy?
>
> No, they aren't.

My eyesight is really bad now, and Dad said I should not watch too much TV. Now, even Patrick started watching on me.

Monday, November 10, 2014

Now, even WITHOUT a broken hand, I am not allowed to play computer games for a year. That is all because of my eyesight. Dad said I couldn't play any computer game until the school checks everyone's eyesight next year. I am really annoyed because I'm still at war in Age of Empires II. And I believe my soldiers would have been crying for my help by now.

Friday, November 14, 2014

We may have a pen thief in our class. Yesterday, one of my friends lost his pen, and today he lost his two new pens. Then we suspected that they had been stolen. In contrast, my stationery has never been stolen. I guess it is because they're too cheap.

Let's look at my pen first. It's just a "thanks for coming" gift from someone's birthday party. And you can make out the difference easily between mine and my friend's pen.

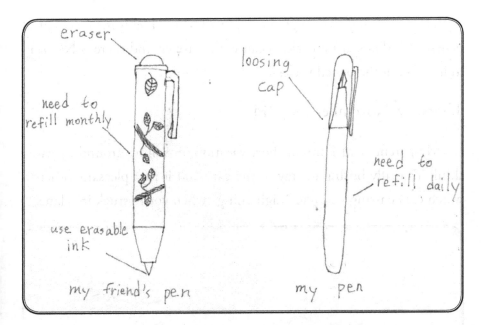

Then, there're the color pencils, but their leads break easily.

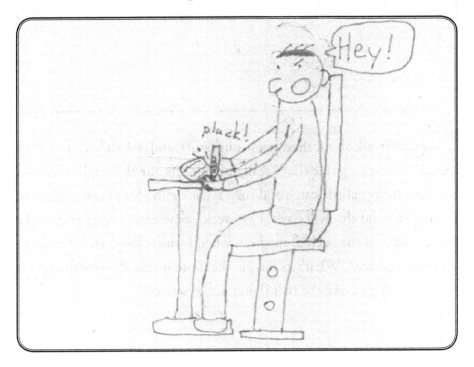

The only thing that might be a target for the thief is my mechanical pencil. But that's just a trick, because it is broken and there is NO lead in it, making the pencil useless.

Thursday, November 27, 2014

My parents and I are on short vacation, travelling around by car. I think it's really boring to stay in the car. And it isn't pleasant either to watch cars passing you like "Lightening" when you're stuck in a lane.

Let's not talk about these depressing stuff, and switch back to school instead. There's a game that's really popular in our class right now and it is something called "catch and snap". The main idea of this game is to catch a ball and throw it back. Last week, some careless guy just fired a ball directly on the back of my head when I wasn't looking. Of course I was very annoyed. What's annoying me more is that the guy thought it was my fault to make the ball flying out of school.

I think I've said that there's nothing to do in Patrick's house, right? Last Saturday I went there again. I put some rocks in the fish tank, to make it more like a pond. But later, aunt came and cleaned all the rocks out. Well, that's what I call a waste of time.

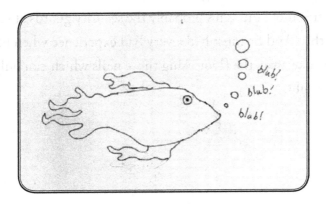

Wednesday, December 10, 2014

I don't know if it's too late to say this, I'm back from traveling. We spent a lot of time in the car, and I spent a lot of time reminding Dad not to drive over the speed limit.

Peekaboo and I built a treehouse this week. Well, today I found that the floor of the treehouse is gone, along with the nails that enable us to climb the tree too! I guess it's probably the security guards at school who had done this. And he must had a very bad experience when he climbed the tree to take away the floor using those nails which can only support the kid's weight.

What was really annoying today was that at the car ride back home, Peekaboo's little brother chomped on my student card, and the card is the most important thing in my schoolbag, because I need it to buy lunch at school! The worse was that he wasn't willing to let it go. A candy may be useful in this situation, but I had no candy at hand.

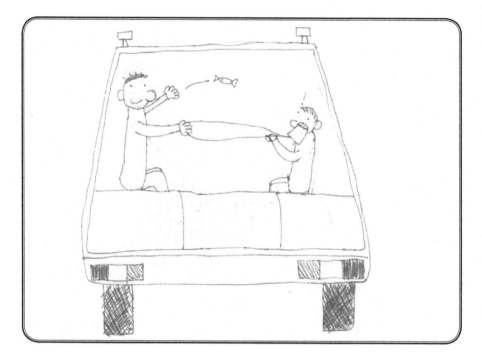

I was worried that the card might be broken if I pulled too hard. So the only possible answer was doing like this.

Thursday, December 25, 2014

Today is Christmas. I didn't write to Santa for gift this year. What at first I wanted from Santa was a remotely controlled helicopter, but then I came to know the accident of my friend's helicopter, which landed on the traffic road.

Anyway, I was still surprised when I saw Santa gave me a handicraft set of Merry-go-round.

Sunday, December 28, 2014

Today Dad, my friend Daniel and I went to the playground to play soccer. Bad luck to me, I kicked the ball too hard and hurt my knee. Just then, Dad called out "Be careful!". The next second, a soccer came landing only a few inches beside me. Maybe my head would had been injured if I had moved a little bit to the right.

I have been thinking of the matters after the publication of this journal, especially worrying about my friends' response if they don't want their names appear in a book. Well, I don't need to worry about this anymore. On the contrary, they said they're gonna kill me if their names won't appear.

Saturday, January 10, 2015

We had the final music test this Thursday. Each student has to sing one song in the test list. The teacher said that each song on the test list cannot be sung more than three times. I thought I would be really lucky, because teachers usually call the students in an alphabet order. The initial of my family name is "D" so I would be the sixth or so in my class to choose the song, which means I could pick those easy songs.

But what I never expected was that this time the teacher decided to count in the opposite way. So don't be surprised when I had to sing those difficult songs in such a high pitch!

Our treehouse was destroyed by a bunch of little kids, and so we're making a garden now. The seeds have been planted for a long time, but I cannot see any progress yet.

Guess it's all because--we forgot it was winter, and the temperature outside is minus two Celsius degree.

Wednesday, January 21, 2015

Today Peekaboo and I had lunch at the canteen in the school. I ordered a plate of fried rice, and there's always some Chinese sauerkraut on it. Well, today there's just some folk behind me must have thought it's his food, and said: "Hey, add some more Chinese sauerkraut!" So then, I saw a whole bunch being placed on my rice. My mouth was almost soured to death after finishing my plate. I really don't have any appetite when peekaboo handed me an orange after lunch.

It made me feel slightly better when Peekaboo came up with a comic book called "Superman and duck". It simply goes like this:

Sunday, February 1, 2015

Bad news! Patrick will stay with us this winter holiday, and I am sure he'll cause lots of troubles. Good news! Grandma scolded him last night. All I know is that it started from not tying his shoelaces properly, and of course many others bad things he committed. Grandma finally made several rules for him to observe.

The interesting part was that I accidentally placed the digital recorder in the living room and switched it on. So it must have recorded the whole conversation between them. Now, whenever Patrick gets naughty, I shall just play the record and all the problems will be solved.

Tuesday, February 3, 2015

Looks like Patrick thinks faster than I do. Today he deleted the record before I take action, which is quite bad. Later he spent a lot of time in playing some English educational games, and that's even lamer than my English homework. In fact, you don't even need to use your brains.

Patrick easily reached the "commander" grade within a week.

Wednesday, February 4, 2015

In order to keep Patrick away during my study time, Grandma asked Patrick to stay in the attic above my study room. Playing computer game is Patrick's quiet time in a day, which can relieve my anxiety about him. But when he plays dominoes, it is usually a disaster. He doesn't use them to build tracks, which is the normal way to play, but giant robots. When those robots fall, it sounds like thundering. I don't know how Patrick manages to adapt himself to this noise upstairs.

I went to Peekaboo's house for a visit today. We discussed about what we shall plant in our garden this winter. The final decision was to plant garlic, but I first need to stand the stink it has.

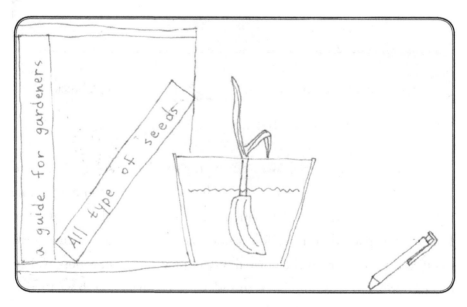

Sunday, February 8, 2015

Aunt bought a copybook for Patrick to practice his handwriting. She also said that he must finish three lines before 2 pm, and he really had a very close call.

Wednesday, February 11, 2015

Let's talk about the dog of our next-door neighbor. I found that the dog really likes to bark. But Patrick also likes to shout out loudly. So he found his competitor here.

He lost the battle for sure.

Sunday, February 15, 2015

We went to the supermarket by car today. I am not interested at all in shopping, but I don't have many choices--I would have to stay home alone otherwise. I regretted it once I knew Patrick would go too. That means a bad and noisy journey was guaranteed.

Thursday, February 19, 2015

Yesterday my uncle said we wouldn't get much sleep last night, because it was the Chinese New Year Eve and boys like me would be very excited. Well, that's very right! With so many firecrackers "cracking" outside, I was still awake at midnight and thought the world was really crazy.

I guess I need to change my sleep schedule from 9pm—9am to 12pm—6:50am.

Wednesday, February 25, 2015

Yesterday Aunt took Patrick and me downstairs to dig some herbs. These herbs are really yummy when being put into Chinese dumplings. When we got out of our building, I cannot believe my eyes: there's a bunch of herbs in our neighborhood! When we collected them, it must have caught the dog's attention, and it started to bark loudly. It might give Patrick a fright, and that's why he picked the herbs cautiously later on.

Patrick likes to build robots. More than that, I find that he has developed feelings on them. When Grandpa accidentally pushed one of the robots down today, the next second he started to bawl like a baby.

Monday, March 2, 2015

The winter holidays are over. Today's news in our class is that our subject representative for Chinese language moved to another city, and I became the new one. My duty is to collect the homework from classmates and hand out the marked one. Well, that's an important but tough work.

Wednesday, March 11, 2015

The garlic in our garden already sprouted. I know that the garlic leaves are edible, so I cannot help tasting a little bit. I really regretted my try. First, it tasted exactly the same as garlic, and that made my tongue on fire. Second, I smelled like garlic all the way home.

Afterwards, I'm seriously thinking about removing the garlic out of our fresh-smell garden.

Thursday, March 19, 2015

One of my classmates unfortunately broke one of his arms recently, so he has to wear the plaster cast. But it is strange to see him in a long-sleeve jacket. When you look him from the back, he looks just like a normal person.

When he turns around, Uh, where is his right hand?

Saturday, March 28, 2015

Now some unfriendly little kids found our garden. Good thing is we know how to climb trees and they don't, so Peekaboo moved the garlic into a flowerpot and hang it on a tree. Bad thing is that the flowerpot had drain holes in its bottom. If you pour too much water, it drips.

What I'm really worried about is that someday the flowerpot may fall down, and I could be right under it at that time.

Thursday, April 9, 2015

The temperature goes like a roller coaster these days. Yesterday I was thinking about having an ice-cream, while today I am thinking about: Brrr ... a cup of hot chocolate will fit me. See what I say?

Thursday, April 16, 2015

In past two weeks, the most important thing is: I created a new imaginary war game played on a paper. It's so awesome that I couldn't even breathe.

You may know the reason after a quick glance of "Game and Map" below. And it is just only a small part of our game.

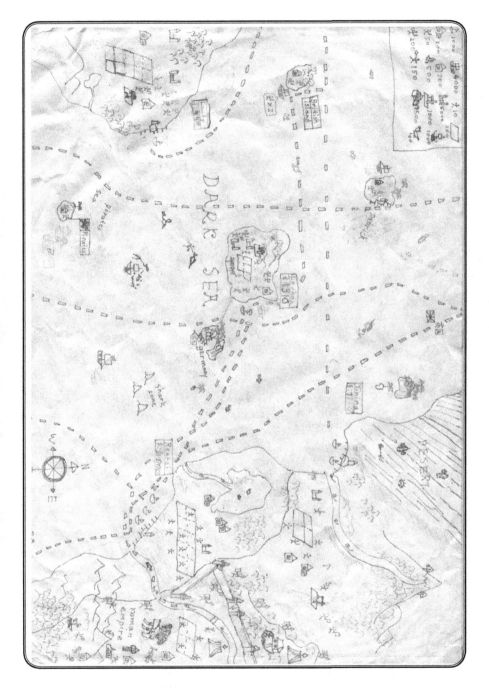

Age of Ding-empires, fighting scenes. Part I.

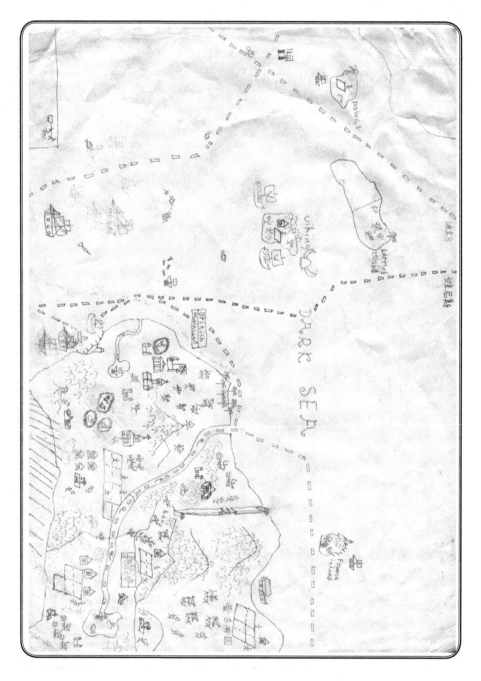

Age of Ding-empires, fighting scenes. Part II.